BON·JOVI

Mick St Michael

WANTED·A·LIVE!

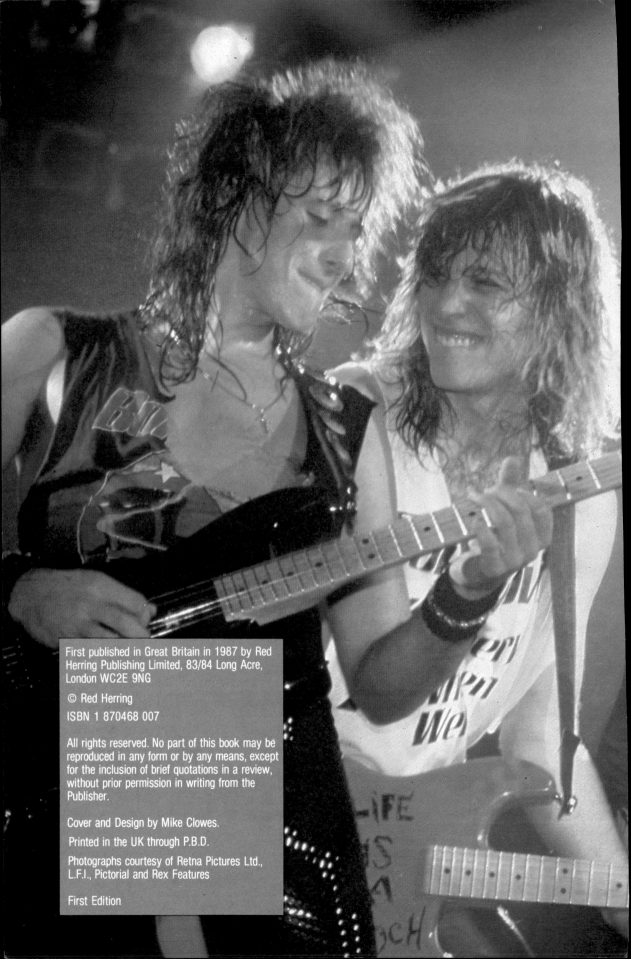

First published in Great Britain in 1987 by Red
Herring Publishing Limited, 83/84 Long Acre,
London WC2E 9NG

© Red Herring

ISBN 1 870468 007

All rights reserved. No part of this book may be
reproduced in any form or by any means, except
for the inclusion of brief quotations in a review,
without prior permission in writing from the
Publisher.

Cover and Design by Mike Clowes.

Printed in the UK through P.B.D.

Photographs courtesy of Retna Pictures Ltd.,
L.F.I., Pictorial and Rex Features

First Edition

BON·JOVI

WANTED·ALIVE!

Mick St Michael

CONTENTS

"The weekend comes to this town/Seven days too soon." No prizes for guessing where *those* lyrics come from – they're the very first words you'll hear as your stylus caresses the 12 inches of vinyl entitled 'Slippery When Wet' . . . but millions of fans worldwide (five million in the States alone) have turned it into purest platinum – several times over! And those self-same fans just wanna rock with their heroes – Bon Jovi!

Bon Jovi, five all-American boys from Bruce Springsteen's backyard, share more than their home with the Boss. They, too, play good-time music with a message – music their fans can identify with on many different levels. It's the kind of music that sounds great in cars, on the coffee-bar jukebox, on the radio in the bath, on the record player at all the best parties – above all, it's music you gotta play LOUD!

But Jon Bon Jovi and his merry men have something even big bad Bruce would consider trading his favourite faded Levi's to recapture. They got the youth, they got the looks, they got the energy of five people who've just hit the spotlight – yet are still hungry enough to want more, more, MORE. Despite the exotic name, this band was born in the USA and the best is undoubtedly yet to come.

PLATINUM HOOKS
If you've only recently had your first fix of Bon Jovi's addictive amalgamation of rock energy and pop hooks, you owe it to yourself to find out more on the band *everyone*'s talking about. Luckily, you're in the right place to do just that . . . after all, you've already missed out on two albums of red-hot rock! And even long-time disciples will enjoy reliving the three brief years when Bon Jovi qualified as the world's hardest-working support act . . . and rock's best-kept secret!

Now all that hard work has paid off, they're a secret no more! Wherever in the world you are, it's more than likely that Bon Jovi have already made a mark on your national charts . . . and brought the weekend that vital bit nearer for their thousands of hard-working fans. As the man says, forget your worries – just 'Let It Rock'!

The house lights dim; the low buzz of excited conversation rises to a crackle, then a hubbub. A few handclaps are heard, a chant of "We want Jon" emerges from the darkened balcony . . . then downstairs a horde of bar-proppers make a desperate charge for their seats – determined not to miss one single second of the band they've come to see.

And they've arrived not a moment too soon! For as the curtains open to reveal a darkened stage, crashing keyboards announce the start of tonight's entertainment. The tune should be familiar – it's 'Pink Flamingoes', the instrumental opening to 'Let It Rock' on the new album. Tonight, though, it's driving the crowd wild . . . they can't see the band, shadowy figures half-hidden behind what looks like a giant Venetian blind.

Bang! Up goes the blind . . . on go the lights . . . crash go Bon Jovi – and the Hammersmith Odeon, London, is on its feet to a man (and woman)! For the next hour and a half, they'd be willing guests at the latest episode of what singer Jon Bon Jovi called "a year-long beach party" . . . and what the critics have hailed as the most exciting live act of the Eighties. But to understand the background to that statement, you have to hitch a Jumbo from Heathrow and head west some 3,000 miles to Newark Airport, New Jersey. The Bon Jovi story, if you like, starts just a stone's throw away . . .

NEW · JERSEY

RUNAWAY

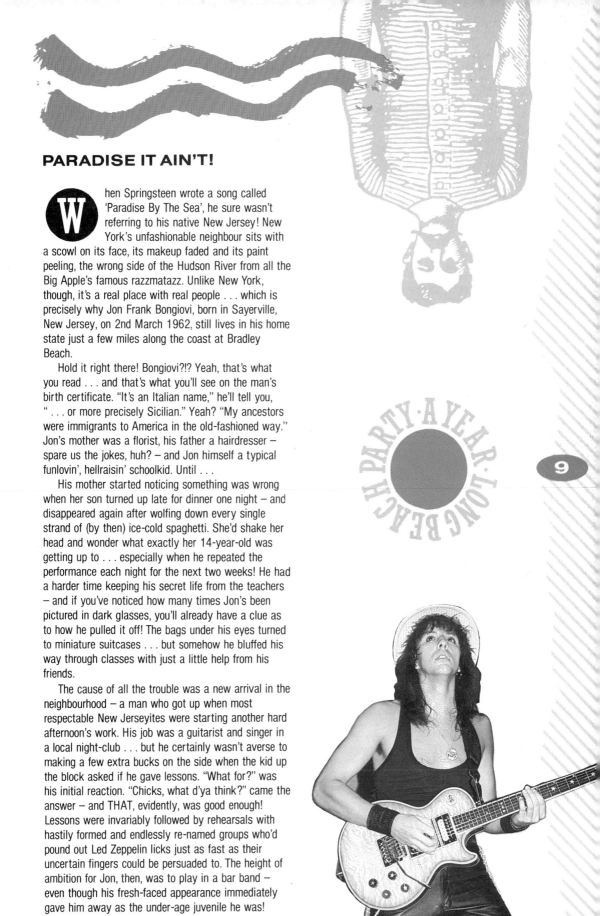

PARADISE IT AIN'T!

When Springsteen wrote a song called 'Paradise By The Sea', he sure wasn't referring to his native New Jersey! New York's unfashionable neighbour sits with a scowl on its face, its makeup faded and its paint peeling, the wrong side of the Hudson River from all the Big Apple's famous razzmatazz. Unlike New York, though, it's a real place with real people . . . which is precisely why Jon Frank Bongiovi, born in Sayerville, New Jersey, on 2nd March 1962, still lives in his home state just a few miles along the coast at Bradley Beach.

Hold it right there! Bongiovi?!? Yeah, that's what you read . . . and that's what you'll see on the man's birth certificate. "It's an Italian name," he'll tell you, " . . . or more precisely Sicilian." Yeah? "My ancestors were immigrants to America in the old-fashioned way." Jon's mother was a florist, his father a hairdresser – spare us the jokes, huh? – and Jon himself a typical funlovin', hellraisin' schoolkid. Until . . .

His mother started noticing something was wrong when her son turned up late for dinner one night – and disappeared again after wolfing down every single strand of (by then) ice-cold spaghetti. She'd shake her head and wonder what exactly her 14-year-old was getting up to . . . especially when he repeated the performance each night for the next two weeks! He had a harder time keeping his secret life from the teachers – and if you've noticed how many times Jon's been pictured in dark glasses, you'll already have a clue as to how he pulled it off! The bags under his eyes turned to miniature suitcases . . . but somehow he bluffed his way through classes with just a little help from his friends.

The cause of all the trouble was a new arrival in the neighbourhood – a man who got up when most respectable New Jerseyites were starting another hard afternoon's work. His job was a guitarist and singer in a local night-club . . . but he certainly wasn't averse to making a few extra bucks on the side when the kid up the block asked if he gave lessons. "What for?" was his initial reaction. "Chicks, what d'ya think?" came the answer – and THAT, evidently, was good enough! Lessons were invariably followed by rehearsals with hastily formed and endlessly re-named groups who'd pound out Led Zeppelin licks just as fast as their uncertain fingers could be persuaded to. The height of ambition for Jon, then, was to play in a bar band – even though his fresh-faced appearance immediately gave him away as the under-age juvenile he was!

FROM SHOES . . . TO STUDIOS!

There were two guiding lights in Jon's life now his confidence with the guitar had outstripped his teacher. One, inevitably, was the Boss, now a chart fixture with his 'Darkness On The Edge Of Town' album. The other was his elder brother Tony, who'd actually been the first in the family to make a living from music. He'd quickly become one of New York's top record producers, working firstly on unfinished albums by the late, great Jimi Hendrix and then with new-wave heroes the Ramones and the Talking Heads. In the near future, he'd find himself co-producing his young brother's first album . . . but for Jon, that vital piece of vinyl was still just something to daydream about.

Instead, he was left to scrape a living by any means a 16-year-old legally could – music still filled his evenings, but wouldn't keep body and soul together. Sometimes, in fact, it threatened to do the exact opposite, as Jon recalls with one particular job. "It was a family shoe store. You had to wear a jacket and tie: my jacket was lime green denim, I wore long hair and sunglasses. Springsteen was playing on the radio and I turned the set way up. People jumped back!" The management wouldn't wear such behaviour . . . and Jon soon got the boot.

Luckily enough, brother Tony came to the rescue, recommending Jon for a staff post at the Record Plant studios in New York City. Not that the assignment was exactly top level . . . in one way, you COULDN'T have got lower! Yes Jon was assigned the ultra-responsible job of floor sweeper – but with an imagination like Jon's a wooden broom handle could easily become a shiny new mikestand!

It was in the middle of one such spell of daydreaming that he bumped – all too literally – into someone who needed an apology . . . but certainly no introduction! Bruce Springsteen was producing an album for Gary US Bonds, and as a result of the chance meeting Bonds recorded Jon's 'Don't Leave Me Tonight'. Bon Jovi was on his way!

RUNAWAY SUCCESS

This was just the inspiration he'd been looking for . . . no more livin' on prayers, it looked like one had just been answered! He'd played Springsteen another song, 'Runaway', which he decided to record himself with the help of E Street Band keyboardist Roy Bittan and some studio musicians called the All Star Review. He then sent the tape to a local radio station. After all, if he'd managed to sell the Boss a song, then disc jockeys should be peanuts, right?

To Jon's amazement, he WAS right! 'Runaway' found itself included on a radio sampler album and earned airplay on no fewer than 15 radio stations the length and breadth of the United States. But Jon had a problem . . . he was on his own again. "I was without a band, without a manager, without a record company. No nothing. Just me."

It didn't prove difficult to find musicians . . . those years on the bar-band circuit had swelled his address book to Meatloaf-like proportions! There was no shortage of willing recruits, either – despite the conditions he laid down. "I told everybody 'No money – we're just going to play for a couple of weeks'," remembers a beaming Bon Jovi. That was four years ago!

Only one of the new boys had previous convictions, so to speak – drummer Tico Torres had played with a vaguely successful Canadian group called Franke and the Knockouts who had, at least, toured the American mainland. Of the rest, guitarist Richie Sambora, keyboardist David Rashbaum and bass-player Alec John Such were local lads aching to make good . . . and they say every great band was once a hungry band!

WHAT'S IN A NAME?

The Mercury record label was willing to write a meal ticket for the new outfit, who took the name of their leader as their own. The subtle alteration in spelling gave them a name that was as easily pronounced as it was difficult to forget – a quality it shared with the music they were starting to make. And when the former floor sweeper walked back into the Record Plant with his brother in mid 1983 – as artist and producer, this time – he had a feeling the last piece of his musical jigsaw had just slipped into place.

"I WAS WITHOUT A BAND, WITHOUT A MANAGER, WITHOUT A RECORD COMPANY. NO NOTHING. JUST ME"

RED HOT AND ROCKIN'

Released in the spring of 1984, 'Bon Jovi' caught the eye – and ear – of even the most casual observer. The front cover showed a pouting, posing Jon keeping an assignation on main street with a foxy lady with legs up to THERE (and few inhibitions about showing 'em!): his four leather-jacketed cohorts posed moodily on the other side. Could it all have been inspired by 'Runaway'? Your guess is as good as anyone's . . . but suffice to say the album became the hottest-selling import item in British record shops on the cover alone! Musically, the band gave an amazingly polished performance, described by SOUNDCHECK reviewer Dee Tracey as 'tight as a Sumo wrestler's G-string'!

Ms Tracey correctly identified 'Runaway' (obviously), 'Breakout' and 'Shot Through The Heart' as the highlights of an uptempo, high-energy set, concluding that "though their material and style can't be called original . . . you'll be itching to see them live." It was typical of the album's favourable reviews . . . but the mean 'n' moody cover artwork, portraying the band as "the best thing since PLAYGIRL – and that's with their clothes on" was to rebound on them later.

OPEN ALL HOURS

So far, so good . . . what was needed now was to get known. Kiss, 38 Special, Ratt, ZZ Top – Bon Jovi opened for 'em all. Even where they were allowed just a six-song set, they'd "hit 'em hard and get the hell out of there. I don't want to bore anybody," said Jon. Some chance! When Bon Jovi hit 'em, they stayed hit – with 'Runaway' the inevitable show-stopper.

With all the touring, it wasn't suprising Jon caught the habit of 'cheating' and taping the name of that night's port of call to his microphone. The album had made Number 43 in the States and Number 71 in Britain . . . even though they'd never played there. So October 1984 saw Jon taping some (to him) unfamiliar names to his mike as they toured the UK with Kiss.

HIT 'EM HARD AND GET THE HELL

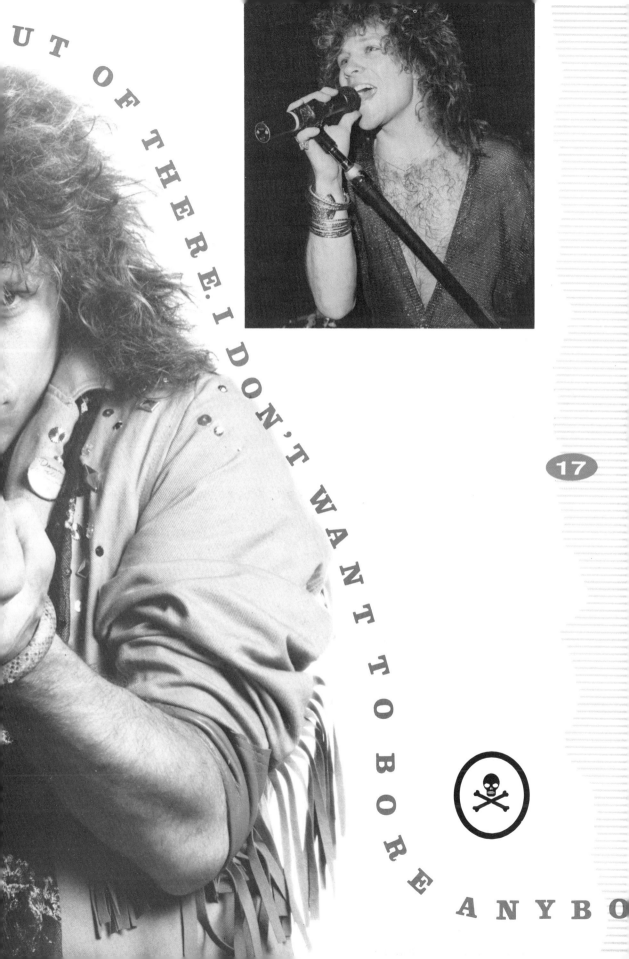

UT OF THERE. I DON'T WANT TO BORE ANYBO

17

Much was expected – by fans and record label alike – when Alec, Tico, Richie, Dave and Jon unpacked their suitcases in Philadelphia to pay their second visit to a recording studio. After all, this was a band at the peak of its form, its musical edge sharpened in front of audiences from Brighton to Boston and all points in between. The title, '7800° Fahrenheit', is the melting point of rock – chosen, says Jon, "to say we were a rock band without being corny . . . with a name like Bon Jovi you don't know if the band's reggae, disco or pop."

'7800°' left no-one in any doubt about THAT! The fans loved it, from the raunchy opener 'In And Out Of Love' (the single that chose itself) to the gentle acoustic guitar, courtesy of Richie, on 'Silent Night'. But even though the album bulleted into the British charts at Number 28, it only made Number 37 back home – due to mixed reviews from journalists who'd labelled Bon Jovi as a good-time rock 'n' roll band full stop. They just couldn't handle the new, introspective side of Jon's songwriting they saw in songs like 'Only Lonely' and 'Silent Night'.

THANKS FOR THE MEMORY

The story behind the making of the album didn't come out until much later – and anyone who'd spotted the 'Special Thanks' credit to one Dorothea Hurley on the first album sleeve might have had a vital clue to the mystery. She and Jon had been split up by the pressures that came with the band's sudden success . . . and it was the strain of their relationship falling apart that gave '7800°' all its sad songs. "It's very painful to call upon sadness as the basis for a song," admits Jon candidly.

But every cloud has a silver lining . . . and when 'Only Lonely' was put out as a single, it joined 'In And Out Of Love' in the American Hot Hundred. "I was pretty messed up emotionally," remembers the singer. "It was a pretty sad song, I guess, but that was the way I felt – and writing is a good way to get my emotions out." Given the rapturous reception 'Only Lonely' wins in live performance to this day, Jon seems to have summed up the feelings of thousands of starcrossed lovers the world over.

TWO'S COMPANY?

Back on the road again, Jon's winning ways with the ladies consoled him somewhat for past disappointments. As he put it, "I've given up being the steady type. I wouldn't trust me on the road with girls – so how could anyone else?" And when photos began circulating that seemed to show Jon enjoying the attentions of no fewer than THREE scantily-clad female admirers, it looked like he was taking his words seriously (sorry, folks – the lawyers just wouldn't let us print 'em!).

They may play hard, but when Bon Jovi work they WORK! And 1985 was the year they brought their music to the furthest corners of the known rock 'n' roll world. In Britain, they played the Monsters of Rock

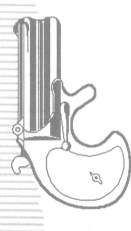

Festival at Donington . . . where someone with a strange sense of humour threw a pig's head on stage! No, the band didn't turn vegetarian – they're the world's biggest consumers of Big Macs, as it happens! – but as Jon said at the time, "it was a dumb kinda compliment."

Prize for the year's biggest stage fright, though, went to the group's showcase concert in May at London's Dominion Theatre, where a PA system failure halfway through 'Roulette' left the band without electricity. Jon picked up his favourite acoustic guitar from the dressing room – where so many lesser singers would've been only too happy to hide – and came out to serenade a hushed packed house with a rendition of a personal favourite from the Tom Petty songbook.

Triumph had been snatched from the jaws of defeat . . . and the finale, with Jon wrapping himself in a Union Jack instead of the usual Stars 'n' Stripes, showed the audience their standing ovation for his earlier showmanship had been more than appreciated. The SOUNDS review of the gig got it right when it commented "This will have been the last time you'll ever pay £3.50 ($5) to see Bon Jovi". A priceless performance in more ways than one!

WRITE ON TARGET!

As his spirits soared, Jon began writing again. Back in the early days, he'd admitted to having to "scrape a bit just to get enough songs together for a complete record. This time, though, I was just spitting them out one after another." One factor in his favour was the partnership he'd built up with guitarist Richie. "We wrote 35 songs, Richie and I . . . then we narrowed it down to 14."

Everyone knew the next album would be make or break. As Jon realised himself, "Some of the songs on our first two albums never quite hit home before they were performed." Live tracks were creeping out on Japanese 12-inch singles . . . and being snapped up at import prices by fans the world over! (See discography.) There were only two possible answers: record a live album (a bit of a risk for a group with only two studio albums to their name) or try to capture the raw energy of a live show in studio performance.

The producer they selected to help them achieve this lofty goal was Canadian Bruce Fairburn, whose studios in Vancouver were far enough away from Bon Jovi's record label to keep well-meaning executives out of their hair. "They'd have had to get on two or three different airplanes," chuckled Jon. No, they didn't want record company pressures – what they wanted was reaction from the kids in the street . . . or at least the local pizza parlour!

"Wherever we went there were about 50 kids hanging out around the place", explains the singer. "So on the last day we took them all back to the studio to listen to the songs – and they told us what they liked and what they didn't . . . it was the best thing we ever did!" The result was 'Slippery When Wet' – the rest, as they say, is history!

23

SLIPPING ● TO ● SUCCESS

No matter how big they eventually become – and there can surely be few limits now – Bon Jovi will never again produce an album that surprised as many people as 'Slippery When Wet'. Facts and figures can be quoted to prove the point, and they could fill an entire book in themselves: let's content ourselves by mentioning that when it hit Number 1 in the American LP charts it gave Bon Jovi the distinction of being only the fifth 'heavy metal' band to do so after Led Zeppelin, AC/DC, Quiet Riot and Van Halen. By its seventh week in pole position, only Led Zeppelin were still in competition!

This was indeed the album that rocketed Bon Jovi into the big league . . . crammed full of potential hit singles and with enough variety of music to keep even the pickiest listener happy. But as many eyebrows were raised by the unusual cover artwork as the record's amazing success. SMASH HITS insisted it was "a wet bin-liner with the title written in the slender hand of Jon Bon Jovi himself" (well, they seem to have got the last bit right, at least!), while rumour has it a naked young lady had been seen pressed up against the shower screen before the censor struck.

The true story wasn't quite as entertaining as the sum of the rumours. "I wanted people to react to the music we were making . . . not the way I looked," explained Jon. The record company DID reject three designs, including a lady in a wet T-shirt (might offend the Moral Majority, y'know!), leaving the band with "about one day to come up with something new . . . it was one step from releasing an album with a blank cover." Maybe someone told Jon he was too late . . . the Beatles beat him to it!

TEN OF THE BEST!

If you've bought this book you'll know the ten tracks on 'Slippery' like the back of your hand. But did you know that 'Wanted Dead Or Alive' was originally going to be the title track because Jon reckons it's "the favourite song I've ever written"? Or that the classic ballad 'Never Say Goodbye' wasn't going to make it . . . until the record company decided there could be ten – not just nine – tracks on the LP? A few months before the album came out, Jon claimed he'd "thrown it in the garbage" – we're sure glad he fished it out again!

The songs that really sold the album were, of course, 'You Give Love A Bad Name' and Richie's voice-box TOUR DE FORCE, 'Livin' On A Prayer'. Both topped the US charts and made the British Top 20 . . . yet they were melodic enough to made radio playlists worldwide. Until 'You Give Love . . .' hit the top, Van Halen claimed America's ONLY Number One heavy metal single with 'Jump'. Move over Dave Lee Roth . . . Jon's on your tail!

So where did Jon and his band go from here? Only the road manager steering them on the next leg of their orbit of the rock 'n' roll globe could tell them . . . But one thing was certain – they were sorry it wasn't New Jersey! "It's still home," claims Jon. "Why move to Bermuda and Miami if you're settled in a place you identify with?" Jon's paid out six months' rent for just two weeks at home – but he reckons every last cent is worth it. Besides, he can hardly be short of the odd dollar these days . . .

They may still live up the road from their roots, but life's undoubtedly changed for these Bon Jovi boys. Jon, for instance, can't get home to sample Mom's pasta as often as he'd like . . . so when the band played London recently he flew his folks out to see them! Another advantage of having his father on the road is that the band get regular haircuts . . . though you might have to look hard to notice the difference with one or two of 'em!

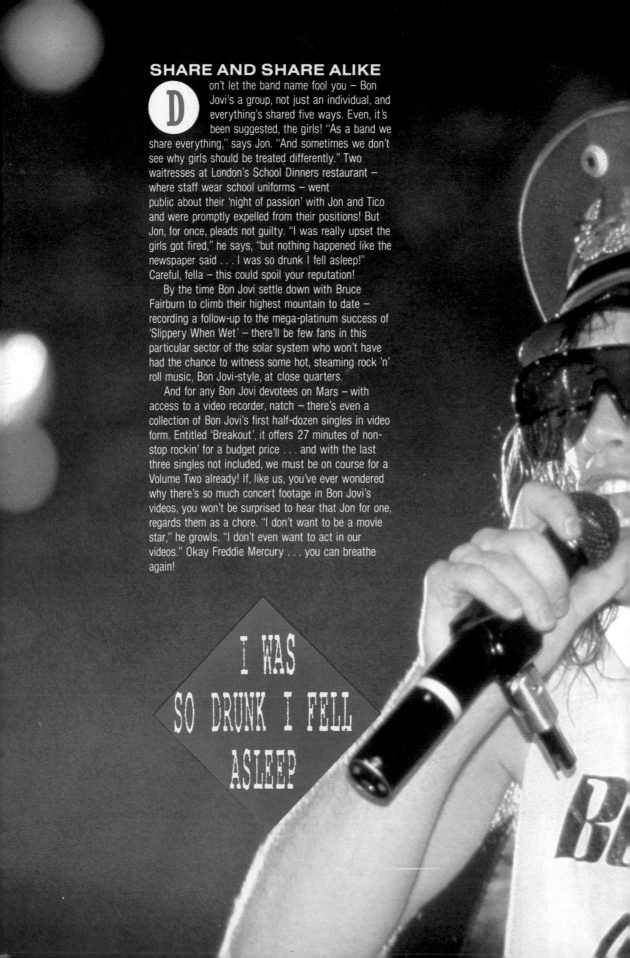

SHARE AND SHARE ALIKE

Don't let the band name fool you – Bon Jovi's a group, not just an individual, and everything's shared five ways. Even, it's been suggested, the girls! "As a band we share everything," says Jon. "And sometimes we don't see why girls should be treated differently." Two waitresses at London's School Dinners restaurant – where staff wear school uniforms – went public about their 'night of passion' with Jon and Tico and were promptly expelled from their positions! But Jon, for once, pleads not guilty. "I was really upset the girls got fired," he says, "but nothing happened like the newspaper said . . . I was so drunk I fell asleep!" Careful, fella – this could spoil your reputation!

By the time Bon Jovi settle down with Bruce Fairburn to climb their highest mountain to date – recording a follow-up to the mega-platinum success of 'Slippery When Wet' – there'll be few fans in this particular sector of the solar system who won't have had the chance to witness some hot, steaming rock 'n' roll music, Bon Jovi-style, at close quarters.

And for any Bon Jovi devotees on Mars – with access to a video recorder, natch – there's even a collection of Bon Jovi's first half-dozen singles in video form. Entitled 'Breakout', it offers 27 minutes of non-stop rockin' for a budget price . . . and with the last three singles not included, we must be on course for a Volume Two already! If, like us, you've ever wondered why there's so much concert footage in Bon Jovi's videos, you won't be surprised to hear that Jon for one, regards them as a chore. "I don't want to be a movie star," he growls. "I don't even want to act in our videos." Okay Freddie Mercury . . . you can breathe again!

I WAS SO DRUNK I FELL ASLEEP

MOVIES AND MUSIC

He may not want to live in Hollywood (or even work there), but Jon's still excited that a couple of his older songs, 'Runaway' and 'Only Lonely', are scheduled to show up in 'Back To The Future' kid Michael J Fox's next movie, 'Around The Corner In The Light Of Day'. And producer Bruce Fairburn still has designs on the 25 songs that never made it onto 'Slippery': Aerosmith wanted 'Social Disease' (but Jon wouldn't let 'em have it!), while even statuesque songbird Jennifer Thrush . . . I mean Rush! . . . is keen to cut a Bon Jovi chewn or two. Jon's quick – TOO quick? – to claim he hasn't heard any of her previous hits. "I know she's sold five million records," he says. "Now apparently she wants to rock 'n' roll". And anyone who wants to rock 'n' roll is alright by Jon!

Something else he's keen on doing is helping other people less fortunate than himself – and Bon Jovi have supported several worthy causes such as Operation Liftoff (a cancer charity), the multiple sclerosis fund ARMS and Farm Aid. Closer to home, he's been helping some of his local bands currently struggling to break out of New Jersey and onto a national stage – a story that's only too familiar from a few years ago. He's already played fairy godfather to a group called Cinderella, having Mercury sign them up and adding some vocals on their Top Ten US album 'Night Songs'. "I got stung by so many people when I was trying to get my first break that anything I can do to help others will give me great pleasure," he says.

I DON'T WANT TO BE A MOVIE-STAR

THE BOYS ARE BACK!

Back at the Hammersmith Odeon, Bon Jovi have finally reached the end of their set. "On the street where you live . . ." sings Jon – and the audience explodes. Yes, it's 'Runaway'! Alec, Jon and Richie give it some heads-down, no-nonsense boogie to the delight of the front stalls, while David's hammering hell out of his keyboards and Tico's powering the whole show as if the evening had only just started! They leave the stage, shaking the outstretched hands, before returning for an ovation and a triple-dynamite encore: 'You Give Love A Bad Name', 'Wanted Dead Or Alive' and a rousing version of Thin Lizzy's 'The Boys Are Back In Town', the cover that's become a calling card for them.

If you've only ever experienced Bon Jovi on vinyl, you owe it to yourself to experience one of their live shows – soon! "I work myself so hard I'll physically bleed for the stage," says Jon. "I want everyone to have a good time at our shows. I want the kid in the 89th row to say 'I swear to God the singer is looking right in my eyes'." You can't ask for more than that . . . so catch these boys – alive!

JON BON JOVI
FACTFILE

Real name Jon Frank Bongiovi
Date of birth 2nd March
Place of birth Sayerville,
New Jersey
Birthsign Pisces
Instruments played Guitar
Previous groups Bar bands, the
All Star Review (the musicians
who cut 'Runaway' in June 1982)
Height 5ft 10ins (1.8m)
Weight 10st 4lbs (65kg)
Educated High School,
New Jersey
Favourite groups Southside
Johnny and the Asbury Jukes,
ZZ Top, Hanoi Rocks
Favourite record 'Bang Bang'
by Sonny and Cher (a US Number
2 in 1966, when Jon was all of
four years old!)
Favourite food Hamburgers –
Macdonalds preferred!
Favourite sport American
Football

"I was a guitar player before I
was a singer but I was the only
guy in the band who could sing
and play guitar at the same time
so I got the job."

Jon employs a lookalike, Texan
model Jim Belling, as a decoy to
keep fans off his trail while on
tour. He gave Belling the month
off when the band last visited
Britain . . . and was promptly
mugged! He signs in at hotels
under various false names: current
favourite is Harry Callahan (Clint
Eastwood's 'Dirty Harry'
character).

A New York radio station ran a
phone-in competition to find the
city's sexiest male. The result? A
tie between Jon and actor Richard
('An Officer And A Gentleman')
Gere. Jon's comment? "That's the
biggest crock of s**t I ever heard
in my life . . . that's not what I
do!"

Jon claims his reputation as a girl-crazy rock'n'roller has become just a LITTLE exaggerated of late. "I'm probably more obsessed with cars than I am with girls," he protests. "I know that sounds a little weird, but cars tend to be totally dependent on you, which is nice!"

Being away from his beloved New Jersey lakeshore may get Jon down sometimes . . . but not for long. Life on the road is definitely for him! "We've busted up bars, got laid in the back of cars and ruined a couple of hotel rooms," he smiles. And why not? As he says, "We're young, we're healthy and we're happy!"

Jon's only regret about his career to date concerns his songs . . . or rather the lack of 'em! "Making music doesn't come that easily to me," he's admitted. "I hear about guys like Springsteen who can write dozens of songs, then choose the best . . . I can only dream about doing that." With 'Slippery When Wet', that dream finally came true!

ALEC JOHN SUCH
FACTFILE

Real name Alec John Such
Date of birth 14th November
Birthsign Scorpio
Instruments played Bass guitar
Previous groups Various New
Jersey bar bands

According to the band's first
record company biography, Alec
John "put in time on the slavish
cover band circuit, doing enough
cover versions of Led Zeppelin and
Judas Priest numbers to send less
stable men over the brink."

When Bon Jovi played New York's
Madison Square Garden as guests
of boogie boys ZZ Top, Alec took a
gun on stage with him, and was
later questioned by police.

He amazed straight-laced British
fans in Bradford last year by
'mooning' to them from the band's
coach as they arrived before the
night's performance . . . and was
stunned to see a female fan take
off her shirt in return. He's
described by Jon as "the Easy
Rider of the band . . . he really
lives the quote 'rockstar lifestyle'."

RICHIE SAMBORA
FACTFILE

Real name Richard Sambora
Date of birth 11th July
Birthsign Cancer
Instruments played Guitar,
piano, sax, trumpet
Previous groups None

Richie was last to join Bon Jovi,
signing on in March 1983 after
seeing Jon in action at a radio
station live broadcast. "This guy in
the audience says to me as I walk
off the stage 'I'm gonna be your
guitar player'," remembers Jon. "I
just laughed and walked away.
But then later I heard the guy play
and the rest is history. I knew I
finally had THE band."

Unlike many rock guitarists, Richie
plays the first solo of each song
"as close as I can to the version
on the record so that you can give
the kids what they're used to
hearing." At the end of each song,
though, "the guys let me break
free and jam – really unleach it!"

Richie has over 30 guitars in his
collection, many with the
distinctive downward-facing
headstock that pays tribute to his
idol Jimi Hendrix (who played a
right-handed guitar upside down).
"I'm so lazy," he says, "that I
don't even like reaching down to
take a guitar out of the case . . .
leave them in strategic places
around the room!"

TICO TORRES
FACTFILE

Real name Tico Torres
Date of birth 7th October
Birthsign Libra
Nickname 'The Hit Man'
Instruments played Drums, percussion
Previous groups Franke and the Knockouts

Tico was spotted by bassist Alec John Such, who drew Jon's attention to the man behind the kit with Canadian band Franke and the Knockouts. They never had a British hit, but sold quite a few albums on import before Tico quit to join forces with the Bon Jovi boys.

The most experienced musician of the five, Tico's earned the nickname 'The Pro' from his mates. "He's made records before," says Jon, "so if I have a question I always talk to Tico about it first."

Bon Jovi's heavy touring schedule suits Tico to a T . . . he simply can't wait to get on stage. "He's always the last guy who leaves the bar and the first one down there," jokes Jon.

DAVE BRYAN
FACTFILE

Real name David Rashbaum
Date of birth 7th February
Birthsign Aquarius
Instruments played Piano, organ, synthesiser
Previous groups Expressway

Classically trained Dave is Jon's longest serving musical cohort, having joined him when neither was legally old enough to drink in the New Jersey bars they played together.

Dave changed his name after recording the band's first album because "it was too ethnic". But he didn't realise that another Dave Bryan already existed – and was on the FBI's hit list for armed robbery! "Every time I check in on a flight, all hell breaks loose," he says ruefully.

Jon calls David "the Indiana Jones" of the group – but Richie simply rates him "an exceptional keyboard player . . . he's the kind of guy who lives the instrument and plays it ten hours a day . . . he just happens to be something else."

FOR THE RECORD

SINGLES

Runaway February 1984 Reached Number 39 in US
She Don't Know Me May 1984 (US only) Reached Number 48
Only Lonely April 1985 (US only) Reached Number 54
In And Out Of Love May 1985 (UK)
Hardest Part Is The Night August 1985 (UK only)
In And Out Of Love August 1985 (US) Reached Number 69
Silent Night January 1986 (US only)
You Give Love A Bad Name August 1986 Reached Number 14 in UK/Number 1 in US
Livin' On A Prayer October 1986 Reached Number 4 in UK/ Number 1 in US
Wanted Dead Or Alive April/ May 1987 Heading for the top at press time!

ALBUMS

Bon Jovi April 1984 Reached Number 71 in UK/Number 43 in US
Tracks: **Runaway, Roulette, She Don't Know Me, Shot Through The Heart, Love Lies, Breakout, Burning For Love, Come Back, Get Ready.**
7800° Fahrenheit May 1985 Reached Number 28 in UK/ Number 37 in US
Tracks: **In And Out Of Love, The Price Of Love, Only Lonely, King Of The Mountain, Silent Night, Tokyo Road, Hardest Part Is The Night, Always Run To You, To The Fire, Secret Dreams.**
Slippery When Wet September 1986 Reached Number 6 in UK/ Number 1 in US
Tracks: **Let It Rock, You Give Love A Bad Name, Livin' On A Prayer, Social Disease, Wanted Dead Or Alive, Raise Your Hands, Without Love, I'd Die For You, Never Say Goodbye, Wild In The Streets.**

CASSETTES AND COMPACT DISCS

Cassette buyers have always had a good deal from Bon Jovi. Aside from the first album (which has a band picture on the inlay), each Bon Jovi cassette comes complete with full lyrics, credits and photos on a fold-out card.

All three Bon Jovi albums are currently available on cassette and compact disc.

WORLDWIDE

Slippery When Wet and the singles taken from it have made Bon Jovi a household name in more countries than we've space to list here. The album has currently topped the US (for a record-breaking eight weeks) and Canadian chart, reaching Number 4 in Holland, 6 in Britain, and 11 in Germany. The singles have gone Top Ten in Britain, the US, Canada, Holland, Finland, Japan . . . you name it! And back with the album, US sales topped the five million mark in January 1987 – just five months after release! These are the fastest sales ever recorded since the multi-platinum awards were introduced in 1984 . . . and the last million passed over the counter in just two weeks. Phew!

VIDEOS

Breakout – The Video Singles (Channel 5). Tracks: **In And Out Of Love, Only Lonely, Silent Night, She Don't Know Me, Hardest Part Is The Night, Runaway**.

COLLECTOR'S ITEMS

Bon Jovi's music has been packaged in many different ways: a selection of the more interesting items are listed below. But hurry! They may not be available for much longer.
Burnin' For Love EP (Phonogram Japan) Features live versions of **Breakout** and **Runaway** recorded live at the Super Rock Festival, Japan, 1984
Livin' On A Prayer double EP (Phonogram Canada) Features unreleased studio track **Borderline**, plus **Breakout, Runaway** and **Shot Through The Heart**, all live recordings.
Slippery When Wet (Phonogram US) Picture disc version available in a limited edition.
Livin' On A Prayer/You Give Love A Bad Name (Phonogram Germany) Double A-side with unreleased studio track **Edge Of A Broken Heart**.
Hardest Part Is The Night (Phonogram UK) Contains bonus live version of **Tokyo Road**.

45

Thanks to Suresh Tolat for help with the discography.